In So Many Words:

A Collection of Interviews and Poetry from Today's Poets

Copyright © 2016 by Madness Muse Press

All rights reserved. Author is sole copyright owner of their work, and retains all rights to the work except for those expressly granted to Madness Muse Press in this Agreement. All work herein belongs to its respective author(s) and cannot be reproduced or used in any manner whatsoever without the express written permission of the respective author(s. Author(s) retain all rights to his/her/their work.

Printed in the United States of America

First Printing, 2016

IBSN- 13: 978-0997859904 (Madness Muse Press)

ISBN- 10: 0997859903

Madness Muse Press
420 Autumn Ave.
Eugene, Oregon

www.MadnessMusePress.com

Madness Muse Press

Table of Contents

Introduction…..7
Michael Collins…..9
Prayer…..15
After High Tide….16
Susan Moorhead…..17
Autarkeia…..23
Bears…..24
Scott Thomas Outlar…..25
Steady in the Storm…..35
Yawning Stars…..37
Gaiyaiobi Xzandis-Zaevan…..38
To My Unborn…..43
Main Character…..45
Julia Klatt Singer…..48
Imagine the world without an alphabet…..55
No angels here…..56
C. Steven Blue…..57
Speed Dreamin'….. 61
Strawberries…..62
Mercy Tullis-Bukhari…..64
Consolation…..71

  Sun.....72

Ingrid S. Kim.....74

  It Grows on You.....78

Victor Clevenger.....80

  A Different Kind of Bad Taste.....86

  Hybrid.....88

Gary Glauber.....89

  Plan, Plane, Planet.....92

  Workshopper.....93

Josh Dale.....94

  Grey..... 102

Gothic Ghetto.....103

  Programming.....107

  The Way of Me.....109

Don Beukes.....111

  African Diva.....118

Marianne Szlyk.....120

  We Disaster Tourists Travel to the Salton Sea.....130

  Let's Go Away for Awhile.....131

Shelly Miller.....133

  Grace.....137

Wesley D. Gray.....138

  Bring the Light.....142

Bilkis Moola…..144
>The Sensory Fairground…..151

Alyssa Trivett…..153
>For a Cup of Coffee…..157

Rebecca Cherrington…..159
>Writer's Tears…..163

Layanne Aman…..164
>Hopelessness…..168

Robert Wilson…..169
>I Can't Party with You Anymore…..173

>Scarlet Brilliance…..174

Ahmad Alkhatat…..176
>I Sat Next to My Life…..179

>I Have Created My Paradise…..182

About the Editors…..185

Adam Levon Brown….186

Claudine Nash….188

Introduction

In the *In So Many Words* collection, the reader will find not just a collection of contemporary poetry, but a series of interviews that grant rare access to the thoughts and experiences of a sampling of today's poets.

The poets featured here may be varied in their craft, but are united in their passion for their art form. They write in the woods, in between their children's Tae Kwon Do classes, in the early morning hours or during the quiet spaces of the night. They scribble down lines at stop lights or write when they walk. They write in their heads or utter lines into their phones on endless commutes.

Some have written for as long as they can recall and have published volumes, others are just beginning their poetic journey. Some are professional writers, others are students, teachers, healers, philosophers or an amalgamation of all of the above.

They write to slow down time, they write not to forget. They write to heal themselves and others. They write to release a mind full of words, to say what they cannot say in conversation, to express the thoughts that burn inside. They write to keep breathing. They write because it is a part of all of them, because they cannot imagine an existence without it.

Join us in reading their words; not just their poetry, but the ones that give us a glimpse into their pasts, their inspirations and the driving forces that have shaped those who live to shape language.

Claudine Nash
Adam Levon Brown

Interview with Michael Collins

Q: When did you start writing?

A: There is historical evidence that I wrote random poems here and there when I was young, and I wrote more and more throughout high school, but I didn't really get "serious" about it until I got to college and had more guidance.

Q: Who are your biggest inspirations/your favorite writers?

A: I spend a lot of time reading non-poets, particularly Jung and those who "dreamed his myth onward" – and various spiritual and scientific influences on his Analytical Psychology. My favorite prose writer is probably Marquez. Or Emerson. Or Twain. Poets: Rilke, H. D., Roethke, Pavese, Berryman, Plath, Gerald Stern, Denis Johnson, Laura Kasischke, Diane Seuss, Ellen Bryant Voigt, Tony Hoagland – a lot more…

Q: What time of day do you do most of your writing?

A: In the morning when I have time to grab a coffee and let my mind Slinky around, or on a walk when I have time to do the same, or on the train when I don't have time and am, therefore, for some reason, all the more productive.

Q: Why do you write?

A: There are plenty or "reasons" I could give for why I write: reflection, self-expression, the joy of creating something, the hope of offering a gift to a reader…but, really, writing is simply a part of who I am. When I don't work on poems for a long period of time, I don't feel like myself, even if I'm enjoying whatever else I'm doing instead. I need the whole experience of creating a poem to be a part of my routine, the spark of connection or insight, the delight of the free write, reflection, revision, agony, the poem's form and content beginning to dialogue, my process of channeling this conversation, the realization of reading it out loud when the poem has become itself. I need all of it.

Q: Do you have any favorite quotes from writers?

A: So many. But I'm assuming you would like me to limit myself to a certain number, which I will stipulate is…four.

"The difference between the right word and the almost right word is the difference between lightning and a lightning bug."

– Mark Twain

"Until you make the unconscious conscious, it will direct your life and you will call it fate."

– C.G. Jung

"When I tell the truth, it is not for the sake of convincing those who do not know it, but for the sake of defending those that do."

– William Blake

"What's madness but nobility of soul / At odds with circumstance? The day's on fire!"

– Theodore Roethke

Q: What is one piece of advice you would give new/aspiring writers?

A: First, make friends with other poets: The dead ones are the most steadfast, but the living tend to be more surprising – and supportive – which is worthwhile from time to time. Second first, make friends with people who are not poets; you always want to be able to have a conversation in which you don't have to remember the difference between synecdoche and metonymy. I guess that was two, not one

Q: Do you have any published books/chapbooks you'd like to talk about?

A: My first chapbook, *How To Sing When People Cut Off Your Head And Leave It Floating In The*

Water, is almost out of print and, therefore destined to be a collector's item. Obviously. And, no, the title poem is not autobiographical.

My first full-length collection, *Psalmandala*, is a romp through the world of esoteric spirituality that includes a diverse collection of new and modified forms and a tonal range that includes comic, surreal, devout, ecstatic and stoical poems, all of which explore the complexities of the soul in their own ways.

My second chapbook, *Harbor Mandala*, is a collection of poems about the harbor near where my family lives in Mamaroneck, NY. The poems explore the boundaries between nature and civilization alongside those between consciousness and the unconscious.

Prayer

Thank you for this sacred gull
        swooping and circling through the noon
blue sky, so my eye could trace

        in his invisible wake
the shape of wind, soul through spirit,
        spirit through soul; it was thunderous

as it approached me – then transfigured
        its visage into a model plane's,
robbed me of the obvious god-

        image I apprehended, returned
the distance I call to you across,
        the between within which I listen.

(first appeared in *The Westchester Review*)

After High Tide

The tide rose over
its confinement, now

from all of this harbor,
from all of the deeper

waters beyond, a small pool
lingers between the break-

water bricks and the sandy
dirt behind them on land.

A remnant, a remembrance,
a separate thing, already

losing itself, slowly being
absorbed by the new

body who holds it.

(first appeared in *Broad River Review*)

Interview with Susan Moorhead

Q: When did you start writing?

A: As long as I can remember there have been words and stories. I have kept journals since grade school, wrote stories and poems and (very bad) songs from high school on. As an adult, I continued to write when I could but it really was put on the back burner as life got very busy. It's only been the last ten years or so where I started sending things out into the world, although not as often as I should.

Q: Who are your biggest inspirations/your favorite writers?

A: A difficult question to put to a poet and writer who is also a librarian happily adrift in a sea of books. Of poets, so many, but I'll start with Adrienne Rich, Anne Sexton, Charles Causley, e e cummings, Naomi Shihab Nye, Billy Collins, Lucille Clifton, Stanley Plumly, Mary Oliver, Nancy Willard, and I have great fondness for the poems in the Corn collections by James Stevenson – wonderful line drawings and observations. I fall in love with new poets weekly, dipping into anthologies and roaming the great used book sales our Friends group at the library holds. The list of writers who inspire me is years long but I would be remiss not to say Virginia Woolf, Alice Hoffman, Elizabeth McCracken, E.B. White, Gladys Taber, Mary Stewart, the Bronte sisters (I read Wuthering Heights a frightening amount of times in high school), and I love a good mystery. I just read a lovely novel, Thomas Murphy, by the writer Roger Rosenblatt is also writes brilliant nonfiction. I read a great deal of nonfiction and recently enjoyed Sy Montgomery's, The Soul of an Octopus. I am currently reading At the Water's Edge by Sara Gruen and Adult Swim, the latest poetry book by Heather Hartley. I also read a copious amount of children's literature and want everyone to wander into a children's library and read all the classics they might have missed along the way.

Q: What time of day do you do most of your writing?

A: I don't have the time to sit at a desk and write mornings or afternoons as often as I would like, but lack of time has made me more efficient in my work habits. I write in my head constantly, scribbling down lines at stoplights, at work, on walks, Poetry is notebook friendly, which is helpful. I was relieved to read how the late poet, Maxine Kumin, said poetry is portable, how she would carry a poem with her in a notebook on errands and work on it while standing on line at the post office or whatever. It's important to me to continually find new ways to work my creative life into my working and home life.

Q: Why do you write?

A: I can't imagine not writing, it's how I navigate the world. Anais Nin talked about writers living in the moment twice – once to live it and once to see it in retrospect. I think the way writers notice things, the way they observe the stories of the world, seek out the right words and rhythms to express what they witness -I feel that's the real gift of writing – that writers get to live their days in a weave of words and images.

Q: Do you have any favorite quotes from writers?

A: I collect quotes from writers and others in notebooks, one of my favorites is from Naomi Shihab Nye, from Salting the Ocean, a poetry collection: "…there may be many things that are too big to write about in their entirety, but there is nothing too small. If you start with something small, it may carry you toward something wider. You are making a map of the days you live."

Q: What is one piece of advice you would give new/aspiring writers?

A: I meet a lot of people who tell me that they want to write but won't or can't because they are afraid of being bad at it or failure. Fear keeps them from expressing themselves in this way that calls to them and that's a shame. I would tell anyone who aspires to write, but hesitates, to resort to all the old tricks – buy crummy notebooks to write in as the fancy ones are too daunting. Set a timer for five minutes and write without ceasing. Write before you get out of bed or before you go to sleep. Do whatever you have to do to honor the voice in your head.

Q: Do you have any published books/chapbooks you'd like to talk about?

A: I have a chapbook that came out late last year called The Night Ghost with Finishing Line Press. I also have poetry and stories in the collections Dogs Singing, Intimate Landscapes, and Somewhere, Sometime.

Autarkeia

The sea does not want or need you.
As you stand gazing out to the horizon's
blur of sky and water, as you cup your hand
to shield an eye from the flares of sun, or
bend to toss that bit of rock into the fingers
of incoming water, as you pocket a chestnut
cowry, a mussel shell bluer than its brothers.

The sea goes about its business whether you
are there or not. The gulls, the only ones to hope,
watch to see if you will be careless and leave a trail
of crumbs to snatch. Beneath the cast of your
shadow, the crab investigates the new discards
of larger creatures stirred up by the small mayhem
of each relentless wave. Already your footprints

are dissolving their gullies of shape on the sand,
imprint of toes disappearing, then arch and heel,
back to a denying smoothness. The waves keep
their continual approach and retreat, the wind its
restless hunt, and you turning over a rubbery clump
of brown kelp in your hands have never felt, as you
often say, more like yourself than when you are by
the sea, this place that holds no claim on you, which
doesn't care if you come or go.

Bears

Younger, I dreamt of bears laying wait in the tall
shadows of impartial trees, the cat glow of their
yellow eyes tracking my movements, patient,
knowing what I did not, about the thick woods,
about the way the night fell quickly in a singular
hush. Hours after waking, the smell of pitch resin
and musk of bear clung in damp patches

to the corners of things, injecting my regular days
with startled boosts of adrenalin, a disjointed
shimmer like sunlight flashing off shards of a
broken mirror, light reeling out in jagged splashes,
patternless, crazed. I dreamt of bears until
I met one, and stood in the rank odor of his
dissimilarity, a paw's length distance,

as he pulled his heft erect and snuffed the cold air
for the scent of my being. I saw the same shaggy
pelt that I remembered, clotted with old berry skins,
bent pine needles, fragments of dried dung. Saw
the same sickening scythe of long claws, but the
small eyes, round and strange to me, dull as old
handled pennies, lacked the fine sheen of the
marauder's intelligence, and I realized I hadn't been
dreaming of bears.

(Previously published in Earth's Daughters)

Interview with Scott Thomas Outlar

Q: When did you start writing?

A: Ye gods! It was such a long time ago that the memories tend to swirl together as a distant, blurred fog. The visions become hazy when I send the neurons back in search of the initial genesis point. But, what the hell, I might as well take a crack at it anyway, eh? I remember sticky, viscous fluids and the foul stench of blood. Despite such hazardous rooming conditions, there was a certain sense of peace that resonated within my spirit at the time. Life was much simpler in those days…every need was provided right at my fingertips. That's it! It must have been around week ten or so when my fingers finally became flexible enough to get down to the business of creating art. In the beginning, it was basically a combination of writing and painting paired together. As I mentioned, the details are sketchy, but from what I can recall, I laced my fingertips in blood (or maybe Mom had just had extra ketchup on her burger that day) and started writing on the walls of the womb. It was a strange form of hieroglyphics that, more than likely, could not be easily deciphered even with modern technology being what it is today. Some people might even argue that those primitive scribblings were pure gibberish. But I say, NAY! There was definitely a solid point being made at the time. I'm damned sure of it. The first sentences went something along these lines: "Get me the hell out of this place! There is a Renaissance Revolution afoot!" I was obviously quite eager to join the fray even at such an early age.

Q: Who are your biggest inspirations/your favorite writers?

A: Well, the list is long, as I'm sure is the case for most artists/writers. When it comes to the written word, scribes such as Hunter S. Thompson, Henry Miller, Joseph Campbell, Hermann Hesse, Charles Bukowski, Jack Kerouac, Joe Casey, Jim Starlin, Roger Zelazny, and Friedrich Nietzsche rank up near the top. Maynard James Keenan, Eddie Vedder, Daniel Johns, Kurt Cobain, and Brandon Boyd are a handful of musicians whose lyrics have sent my mind swirling through the years. Honestly, these days I'm nearly completely consumed by contemporary poetry, but I won't start listing names here because I'd likely leave off dozens of people whose work I admire…and then I'd feel like a royal jerk. However, if you check out my blog at my site 17Numa you can find links to the websites, archives, and publications of many such folks who inspire me on a regular basis.

Q: What time of day do you do most of your writing?

A: Sweet Jesus, that's a hard answer to nail down because, truthfully, the compulsion to bleed ink never seems to fade throughout the day. I keep a pen and paper with me at all times should inspiration happen to strike at any given moment. Sometimes I'll wake up first thing in the morning and kick things off immediately by writing down my dreams (this, of course, is predicated upon remembering such imagery…which can sometimes be a tall order depending upon the previous night's activities). I enjoy walking up to the local park each afternoon where I'll hammer out a poem or two in the woods. This is probably the closest thing to an official routine that I have. We all have our habits, I suppose. Writing happens to be the healthiest of mine. The others, in all fairness, while perhaps not being good for the internal organs, do still tend to help the words pour forth. I won't go into the specific details here. It just wouldn't be prudent. It's important, after all, to leave some things up to the reader's own imagination.

Q: Why do you write?

A: I noticed that not many other people tend to participate in such an activity. There seemed to be a vacuous void crying out to be filled. I just can't explain why the craft hasn't quite caught on with the masses yet. I jest, of course. The market is obviously saturated to the point of rupturing in an explosion that would rival the Big Bang. Maybe that's the key right there. Much of life bores me to tears, so I've always enjoyed a good challenge to make the experience a bit more exciting. Trying to have one's voice heard amongst a crowd of millions seemed like a course of action that was right up my alley. Now, with all that being said, let me offer the politically correct, canned response that one is supposed to give: I write because my soul demands it. It's a natural urge that is born deep in the fiery abyss of my bowels. I just wouldn't know what to do with myself otherwise. Writing is the expression of my truest, most unique, special snowflake self.

Q: Do you have any favorite quotes from writers?

A: I do, indeed. Depending on my mood, I could answer this question in a hundred different ways. Here are a few that come to mind in this particular moment:

Hunter S. Thompson from "Fear and Loathing in Las Vegas" –

"All energy flows according to the whims of the great Magnet. What a fool I was to defy him."

Fyodor Dostoyevsky in the opening lines from "Notes from Underground" –

"I am a sick man…I am a spiteful man."

Joseph Campbell –

"Follow your bliss and the Universe will open doors for you where there were only walls."

Friedrich Nietzsche from "Thus Spoke Zarathustra" –

"But the poets lie too much."

Q: What is one piece of advice you would give new/aspiring writers?

A: Be true to your own inner compass. Don't rely on the praise or adulation of other people to determine the worth of your writing. Be inspired by and learn from those figures who you draw inspiration from, but do not mimic their style or voice to the point where you lose all sense of originality. Such a course of action is tacky and gross. Rejection is part of the process. Be prepared to stand back up and steel your will with a steady resolve each and every time you get knocked down. Editors are not out to get you. Their job is difficult (I'm learning this first hand more and more as I get deeper into such efforts myself). If your work isn't a fit in one particular venue, it doesn't mean it might not be a perfect match elsewhere. Research and know the markets you're submitting to so you aren't wasting anyone's time, including your own. If your work does happen to get rejected, understand that it isn't a personal attack against you (well, in all honesty, sometimes it might be…but this usually won't happen until later on down the line after you've ruffled enough feathers to become considered "problematic" in certain circles because of your provocative nature). Read as much as you possibly can...and when you're not reading, write, write, and write some more. Keep your eyes on the prize and stay committed to your craft for the long haul. That was obviously more than one piece of advice. Admittedly, I've never been good at playing by the rules.

Q: Do you have any published books/chapbooks you'd like to talk about?

A: My most recent chapbook "Songs of a Dissident" was released in December of 2015 through Transcendent Zero Press and is now available on Amazon. The work was recently described thusly by Sunil Sharma in a review he published in Tuck Magazine:

"Building a reputation of a young dissident through his widely-published poems, Scott challenges the lies and questions the official version with the probity of a seasoned lawyer or journalist. Very few poets these days do this job of a compassionate dissident, critical of the power structures and other dominants. The State, of course, is wary of such a hatchet job. But Scott does not care; he willfully takes on the system in his poetry. His sole concern is revealing the truth behind government-speak and deceptions being circulated in the name of administration and governance, supported by the mass media."

I'm also very excited about two forthcoming poetry collections that are in the works. "Chaos Songs" (Weasel Press) and "Happy Hour Hallelujah" (CTU Publishing) are set to be released later in the year. More information about both projects will be coming soon.

Anyone interested in finding out more about my work can visit 17Numa where links to all my published poetry, fiction, essays, and interviews can be found. With that, I'd like to close things out by saying thank you for providing this platform where I could ramble for awhile. What you've been doing for the literary community of late with all your hard work is very much appreciated. Selah

Steady in the Storm

Lightning strikes
sirens roar
dogs howl
cats scream
children sleep soundly
and it is beautiful

Fire starts
graves yawn
ants march
wasps sting
children laugh heartily
and it is beautiful

Wars rage
jihadists bomb
cancer comes
bones rot
children play in the streets
and it is beautiful

Men cheat
women lie
marriages crack
love dies
children dance with their imagination
and it is beautiful

Chaos consumes
darkness reigns
world collapses
God resigns
children hold down the fort
and it is beautiful

Yawning Stars

I watched you yawn a universe into existence
I witnessed as you sang a cosmos into style

I saw you sigh, and the heavens roared
then you smiled, and the gods came alive

I felt you move, and the stars fell into rhythm then
you danced, and the planets cycled into their place

You closed your eyes, and the full moon shined
and when they opened, the sun blazed hot

Your passion flared, and the earth shook violently
but then you laughed, and all grew calm

You said Yes, and the gates flew open
Your power coursed through every wave

You spoke the Word, and the gospel was born
Your vibration, a serenade of the holy symphony

Interview with Gaiyaiobi Xzandis-Zaevan

Q: When did you start writing?

A: Honestly, I have been writing since I was about seven. It started out as quirky stories but I would always trash them. Then I recall writing stories with a classmate when I was around ten. We would trade stories like the cartoon crime shows we saw on television. We made up characters and everything. I used to write poems when I was little but discard them as fast as I wrote them. Until I was about seventeen . That's when I just started writing and cataloging my poems. That's when I became a serious poet/writer.

Q: Who are your biggest inspirations/your favorite writers?

A: I have so many writers that i adore. Alice Walker, Maya Angelou, Langston Hughes, Oscar Wilde, Jane Austen, Anthony Trollope, Charles Simic, Raymond Carver, Martin Amis, Saul Bellow, Gabriel Garcia Marques, Borges, Cortazar, Junot

Diaz, Ashley & Jaquavis, and Meesha Mink/Naiobi Bryant and many more.

Q: What time of day do you do most of your writing?

A: There are no particular hours for me. They generally vacillate from wee night hours to random busy hours within the day.

Q: Why do you write?

A: Writing is part of my everyday life like breathing, seeing, smiling, It is, and has been, therapeutic, revealing, and entertaining. Writing has helped me evolve into the quality human being that I am today.

Q: Do you have any favorite quotes from writers?

A: I have several actually. I am a fan of three quotes in particular by Oscar Wilde, J.D. Salinger, and Alice Walker.

Walker's quote is the shortest: *"Expect nothing. Live frugally on surprise."*

Oscar Wilde's is from the essay De Profundis. There was so much to like about his essay but this quote is the best to me: "The final mystery is oneself. When one has weighed the sun in the balance, and measured the steps of the moon, and mapped out the seven heavens star by star, there still remains oneself. Who can calculate the orbit of his own soul?"

And lastly is Salinger's from his story Franny & Zooey: "There's an unwritten law that people in a certain social or financial bracket can name-drop as much as they like just as long as they say something terribly disparaging about the person as soon as they've dropped his name—that he's a bastard or a nymphomaniac or takes dope all the time, or something horrible."

Q: What is one piece of advice you would give new/aspiring writers?

A: Honestly I would tell writers to focus on developing their own voice. Don't try to be the next Shakespeare or Ginsberg or Angelou or fellow rap star/spoken word celebrity. Just do you and find your voice, your passion and let the creativity flow.

Q: Do you have any published books/chapbooks you'd like to talk about?

A: I have an ebook entitled Naïve Eve: A Novella. It will be available in print format this year as a twin novella entitled Naïve Eve/Maceo Desaint. Also, I have a poetry book in the process of being published entitled Drive:Poems. I hope people will read and enjoy them.

To My Unborn

I feel you

Staring at me

With a perplexed incredulity

about my life and

the idea of happiness.

My thoughts eye –

From periphery to

a complete stare

commands the neck,

head to bend in your

direction.

You –

I fancy -

meet my stare

with

Solemn, peaceful bewilderment

then u mouthed

a slant whisper,

"thank you."

As I ponder how

fragile we are

in spite of our cruel nature,

I wonder.

Yes I wonder.

The shape of our hearts;

Our individual hearts.

Better yet, the shape of

  emotions;

a collection of our individual

  emotions,

In the wake of a reality

  commanding us,

To perform *audible* plays

  to survive.

Main Character

Learning

Not to worry

about

can-nots

for it may

        cut

one's life short-

shorter than it already is.

No time

to waste on

feeling neglected

by someone

        or something.

No-no.

no time

to waste on

such frivolity;

jealousies,

false fronts, other deceits

and unkind acts

for it may

        cut

one's life short –

shorter than it already is.

Enjoying

a freedom

of rich experiences

without those pesky gnats;

jobs, bills,

their collectors

oh yes

some main character

stranded somewhere, perhaps

Seeking? Finding balance:

Listening to the smile of the wind.

Seeing   the glow of warm

thoughts

Cherishing today's moments

Cuz tomorrow may come, it may not.

Interview with Julia Klatt Singer

Q: When did you start writing?

A: If you asked my mother, she'd tell you when I was three I walked around rhyming all the time, then moved on to stories. I do remember walking home from school and telling myself a story as I went, often arriving home and be surprised I was already there. But I didn't start writing, really writing, until after I'd be a high school teacher for six years. I was teaching social studies and decided to go to graduate school, focusing on art and literature since I was teaching the A.P. European classes. I needed one more credit that first fall semester and I took a short story writing class on a whim. And that pretty much began my life as a writer. I didn't go back to teaching social studies, instead, after writing for a couple years and getting published, I became a rostered artist through Compas and began my dual life as a writer and a teaching artist.

Q: Who are your biggest inspirations/your favorite writers?

A: There are so many. Eudora Welty, Raymond Carver, Li-Young Lee, Haruki Murakami, Tom Waits, Pablo Neruda, Bob Dylan, Emily Dickinson, Nazim Hikmet, Tolstoy, Dostoevsky, and Hemingway.

Q: What time of day do you do most of your writing?

A: I write when I have the space and time to write. So some days that is mornings; others, night. In many ways, I am always writing, carrying some line in my head, following some bird, waiting for rain. Writing requires the getting it down, but it also requires the finding it, the openness to it. It isn't something I can force. It isn't a job I clock certain hours for. It is just what I do.

Q: Why do you write?

A: I think originally I started writing so I wouldn't forget things. People, images, incidents, things told to me. And I still write to remember, but I think too,

I write now to make sense of the world. Not the whole world, but my small piece of it. My small part in it. And even though this isn't working, I think I write to slow time down. If I am paying attention to the way the light flickers through the leaves of trees, or the way the moon climbs out of the branches, I am there, alive, in that moment and poem too. My father collected butterflies and moths when I was a girl. It made me sad that they were dead, pinned on long thin pins with colored enamel heads to cork and cardboard. But you could see them; see their bodies, the wings and underwings. Their thin antenna. Their thinner yet legs. Sometimes I think my poems are like that, a pinning down of time and feeling so that we can see it.

Q: Do you have any favorite quotes from writers?

A: This, from Hemingway, "It was necessary to get exercise, to be tired in the body, and it was very good to make love with whom you loved. That was better than anything. But afterwards, when you were empty, it was necessary to read in order not to think or worry about your work until you could do it again."

Meaning, for me, that you have to live your life. That writing is a part of it, a very essential part of it, but it is not all you do, or should do. Keeping the worry at bay is important. Because there is so much to worry about when one is writing (if it is any good, if it makes sense, if it will add up to anything at all, if anyone else wants to read this, if you should be doing something else, something less solitary and punishing, something useful, if anyone really like what you write, or if everyone is just humoring you, being kind) and the worry is never helpful to the writing.

Q: What is one piece of advice you would give new/aspiring writers?

A: Write. Write and write and write. Then be brave and share it with someone. Then someone else.

Share it with people you know and people you don't know. Read it out loud. You'll hear then what works and what doesn't. What need more and what needs less. Then write some more. It isn't about pleasing everyone. It isn't competitive. It is writing until you've done it justice. And then you let them go off and be poems and stories. They aren't you. They are just something you do. Keep doing it. Write and write and write.

Q: Do you have any published books/chapbooks you'd like to talk about?

A: I have three books of poetry published: A chapbook called *In The Dreamed of Places*, (2012) published by Naissance Press, *A Tangled Path to Heaven* (2013) and *Untranslatable* (2015), published by North Star Press. I am also co-author of *12 Branches: Stories from St. Paul*, Coffee House Press, (2003)

I also have co-written a number of songs with Composers Tim Takach and Jocelyn Hagen.

Somewhere in the range of 9 to 15 with each? I've kind of lost count. In many cases they are writing from a poem I've written, so they just ask for my permission to use the poem as text. But I have also been commissioned to write poems for them to set to music. Yesterday I heard *Everything Sings* sung by a choir of 250 children ages 7 to 18. This was a poem Tim had me write for the choir's 35 anniversary. And Jocelyn and I have the title song of the Houston Symphony Choir's latest album, *The Soft Blink of Amber Light*, based on a poem of mine, *How To Live in the Modern World*.

Imagine the world without an alphabet

Noise that can't be named,
Names that we will never learn
Or remember, yours, on the tip of my tongue.

To cope, our thoughts take the shape
Of fruit and the moon,
Cloudy drawn lines,
Not that we can explain that
To ourselves
Or to each other.

All I can do is
Press my thumbnail into the skin
Of an orange, peel it
(the scent of orange in the air)
Pull it apart, piece by piece & place
A slice on your tongue.

All I can do
Is study your body
How it moves and holds the light
How your eyelids quiver
How long you hold it, and when
you swallow.

No angels here

No trees either
except for the stand of them
that used to protect
the now fallen farmhouse
from the wind.
The house is gone,
the wind remains. The road
is still narrow, rutted, rock and
dirt. Looking into the rearview mirror
the message is clear:
No use looking back
if you do
you're not going to see much
until the dust settles
and even then
it's just a narrow road
one you traveled down
and there's enough dust
in your lungs, tucked in the seams
of your clothes, and your car
to remind you
of who and where
you've been.

Interview with C. Steven Blue

Q: When did you start writing?

A: I won my first poetry award when I was 12 years old.

Q: Who are your biggest inspirations/your favorite writers?

A: Inspirations: John Lennon, Bob Dylan, Neil Young, Joni Mitchell, Jimi Hendrix.

Favorite writers/poets: Rod McKuen, Bernie Taupin, E.E. Commings, Robert Frost, William Stafford

Q: What time of day do you do most of your writing?

A: Late night or morning.

Q: Why do you write?

A: It has just poured out of me since I was a kid. But, also, as a release, to express what I cannot say in conversation.

Q: Do you have any favorite quotes from writers?

A: You may say that I'm a dreamer, but I'm not the only one.

Life is what happens to you while you're busy making other plans.

Q: What is one piece of advice you would give new/aspiring writers?

A: Don't quit. No matter what, pursue your dream.

Q: Do you have any published books/chapbooks you'd like to talk about?

A: The Wordsongs series / S.O.S. Songs Of Sobriety

To see more information about these books, go to the following links:

The Wordsongs
Series: www.wordsongs.com/wordsongs1

S.O.S. Songs Of
Sobriety: www.wordsongs.com/sos

Speed Dreamin'

Two voices drift softly
on the winter breeze.
The heater crinkles in this
weather as it awakens me
from the dream of writing you
        a poem,
you soft, moist-kissing redhead:
theatre goer of another past dream.

You read me the ratings
of previous lovers—the entry is mine
and I attempt to write you
        the poem
of a young girl, sound effects and all,
zooming down the hill
in a yellow boxcar racer.

Strawberries

Ever since we've met
I've had this strong urge
to eat strawberries
  fresh
    nourishing
      effervescent

Each kiss
like a snowflake's
unique pattern floating
  softly
    in the air
      then landing

Each a small
but integral part
of a soft
  white
    fluffy
      feather-bed

Each but a small
patch
in the quilt
  becoming
    our life
      together

One full of days

fresh for picking
strawberries
 you are
  still blossoming

   on the vine

Interview with Mercy Tullis-Bukhari

Q: When did you start writing?

A: I can't even remember when I started. For as long as I was able to write, I wrote stories and poems. I even experimented with writing rap lyrics when I was in elementary school.

I recall instances of violent arguments between my parents. At some point, my spirit—my higher self, that abstract but prominent entity that we all have—led me to words. My spirit knew that words would help in my emotional and mental survival, in a space where the adult figures in my life were not presenting a serene and peaceful home life for me. Yet, the physical aspect of my existence took a bit longer to catch up to my spirit.

Four years ago was when I took my writing very seriously. I was in a place where I was looking to feed my soul, and the life I had then was not fulfilling. Referencing Bob Marley, my belly was full but I was still hungry, you know? I was pushed to get a degree, get a career, and to not "waste" my time with writing. When I took my writing more seriously, was when I felt I was living a life that matched who I was. Writing initially was this thing that I always secretly enjoyed. But let me tell you, since I have welcomed writing, I have definitely been fed. When I truly allowed my writing to feed me, was when I became born as a writer.

Q: Who are your biggest inspirations/your favorite writers?

A: Georgia Douglas Johnson rocks. She was an important poet of the Harlem Renaissance who has not gotten as much attention as the other poets of that era. The American Literary Canon minimally acknowledges the Harlem Renaissance, and even less so for the important woman poets of that time. She was a classically trained musician, so many of her pieces are very much like songs, with rhythm, rhyme, and beat. For instance:

I want to die while you love me

And never, never see

The glory of this perfect day

Grow dim or cease to be

The lines above read somewhat like a nursery rhyme. She was a very passionate poet, very much in love with love and life, and her poetry shows her dedication to the art.

Lately, I have been devouring Tracy K. Smith. Her other-worldliness in her writing yields to unexpected but realistic interpretations of life events.

Junot Díaz made being bilingual in my writing acceptable, without footnotes and explanations.

I read *On Writing* by Stephen King regularly. I actually listen to the audio recording many mornings when I am doing my few minutes on the treadmill.

My writing godparents (in my head, anyway) are Toni Morrison and William Faulkner. I appreciate the way they are able to so beautifully reflect the way our thoughts and our consciousness function.

And, finally, my uncle (also in my head) is James Baldwin. His brilliance is admirable, and I aim to infiltrate intelligence into my writing the way Baldwin has.

Q: What time of day do you do most of your writing?

A: As a full-time mom, I try to get a few minutes here and there. I don't have that luxury (or the discipline, honestly!) of setting aside an hour or so to sit and write. I keep my Moleskin and iPhone with me at all times, so when inspiration hits (whether it is in the car waiting for my kids to come out of school, or during my daughter's dance lesson, or during my son's Tae Kwon Do class-I am reading and/or writing, utilizing the minutes I have to do my art.

Q: Why do you write?

A: I write because I need to live.

Q: Do you have any favorite quotes from writers?

A: "I love my rejection slips. They show me I try." Sylvia Plath

Q: What is one piece of advice you would give new/aspiring writers?

A: Stay persistent, and get yourself published. Not many of us will be as lucky as Emily Dickinson. The bulk of her poems were published after her death. As writers, I believe in leaving a legacy, a written representation of who we are as individuals and as a society. We have so many options to put our work on print now. Publishing outlets are not as elusive now as they were at least ten years ago. Someone will publish you; if you don't get published, you can always publish yourself.

Also, you must, must, MUST consistently and constantly hone your craft. Regardless of how good you are, you must always allow yourself to grow as a writer.

Q: Do you have any published books/chapbooks you'd like to talk about?

A: My first book of poetry is called *Smoke*, published by Blind Beggar Press, Inc. A print and digital version are available on Amazon.com, and signed copies are available on Etsy. I can be found on many of the Blind Beggar Press, Inc. anthologies as well. I am also an essayist, and will have an essay published in the 2017 Women of Color Anthology: *All the Women in My Family Sing*. Of course, I had to partake in a Prince tribute anthology somewhere, so I am grateful that Yellow Chair Review recently published my poem in their anthology, *Only Wanted to See You Laughing*.

Consolation

I admire the resilience of the strong—
The ability to creep through a tornado of packed
duffle bags
With the calm of a fed baby.
For me, the insistence of where to go from here,
Barely creeps into my petty cobweb of a brain.

I stand in front of my severed head—
A portrait. You, the artist,
With remnants of the red paint on your wicked right
hand
Waving to receive accolades for the
Masterpiece of my dripping head.

A pat on my shoulder once,
Like the reassuring but condescending pat
a little league baseball player gets
when he misses the tie-breaking catch.

A caress between my legs before,
In hidden parental closets and
red-sheets, Jerome Avenue hotels.

I will always have affection for you.
You will always be my first love
You will always be my girl
You say, while cupping the breast of that person
You call your woman.

Sun

There you are—
Peeking from the east
Creeping up steadily
Removing the cloak of
yesterday's shadows
And regrets.
Sprinkling the land
With the new day of light.

There you go—
Up, riding up the sky
Like the first incline of the Cyclone
Filling the blessed of those who
Opened eyes today
With the desire to
Wrap arms around
A palette of new experiences.

There, you—
Cradling my carriage of fear,
Ridden by horses into the
Constellations we will see
When you leave—
And the constellations will stay
Like reminder notes of party
Of yesterdays

That will revive
When you arrive again.

Interview with Ingrid S. Kim

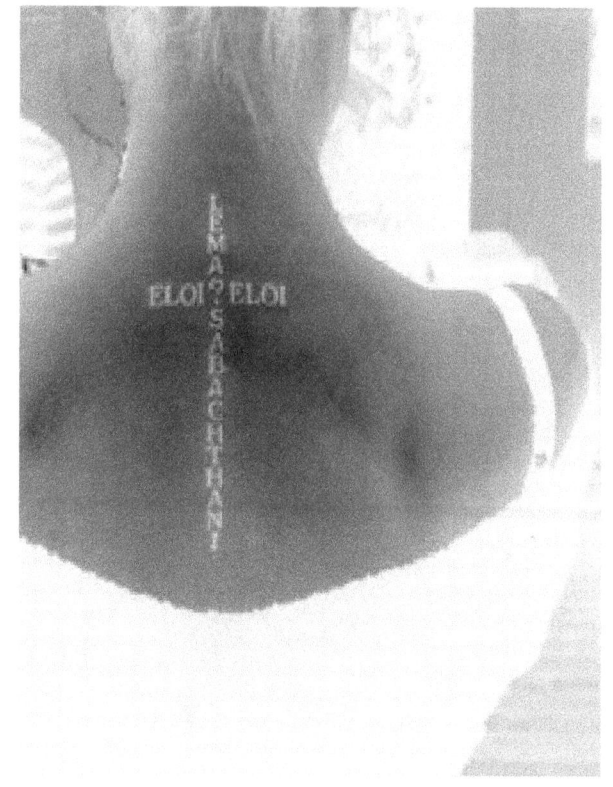

Q: When did you start writing?

A: I remember writing terrible poems around 10-11, I might even still have a few of them in a drawer somewhere. During junior high school, I used to write love letters on behalf of classmates, it was hilarious to initiate love stories between them having written all the letters they exchanged. I always loved essay time in school, then growing up I found it easier to explain things with a pen and a piece of paper than verbally, I guess writing has been my way of both expressing what matters and understanding the world ever since I learned how to. I started writing more seriously in my twenties, published in various magazines and collections in France and in the US for a few years, and my first personal collection in France was finally published last year.

Q: Who are your biggest inspirations/your favorite writers?

A: I am an obsessive reader; it is a very hard question, as I love so many different genres and writers, from Stephen King to Borges, from poetry to fantasy or sci-fi, from philosophy to mysteries, biographies, History... I have to mention Jim Morrison, as a poet, not as a rock star, as he's the one responsible for my will to learn English and understand what he was saying when I was around 14, and then Bukowski, Emily Dickinson and Robert Frost, among so many others, for making me fall deeper in love with poetry in English.

Q: What time of day do you do most of your writing?

A: Whenever I can, actually... but I always preferred night. Cliché right?

Q: Why do you write?

A: To keep breathing.

Q: Do you have any favorite quotes from writers?

A: "To be a poet is a condition, not a profession." (Robert Frost).

Q: What is one piece of advice you would give new/aspiring writers?

A: Do not compromise. Ever.

Q: Do you have any published books/chapbooks you'd like to talk about?

A: For wandering French speakers, my collection "Déambulations" is available worldwide. In English, among others, you can find a couple of my poems in Michael Lee Johnson's anthology Moonlight Dreamers of Yellow Haze, and I'll be featured in the upcoming Shattered anthology from Kind of a Hurricane press.

It Grows On You

It grows on you
Making your twenty-year-old self
Moan in agony
First time you tell your friends
Sorry guys I have plans
And as you curl up in your blanket
Reading poetry out loud to your purring cat
You whisper for yourself only
Plan of week
Indeed
Or wallowed in your couch staring blankly
At yet another crime show
On the TV screen
And the archetypal hero
Blue eyes and AA chip in his left pocket
Gets this close to lose it to
Jim Beam
Again
Or to the hooker with the pretty eyes
First time you want to bark at him
Come on man
Don't
Just
Don't
Instead of calling him a pussy
First time watching that old Disney movie with your
Best friend's kids
The one with the annoying mermaid

You know
That time when she screams at her Dad
I ain't no kid anymore I am
Sixteen
And you burst out laughing
Damn right you're a kid young lady
Tail or not
Now piss off and go clean your room
Or whatever it is called
Under the sea
First time
Your banker calls you missus
First time you wake up on a Sunday
And your head is just okay
First time you write
Sober
And it ain't that bad and it's just
Enough
For the first time

It grows on you
The peace
At last

But that sour taste in your mouth

Interview with Victor Clevenger

Q: When did you start writing?

A: Thirteen, or fourteen; shit, it was around there. I always kinda remember having an obsession with words, but the poetry started when I began sneaking Bourbon, Vodka, and cigarettes into my grandmother's house at nighttime. I would drink it and listen to Snoop, Biggie, The Doors, Bob Seger, and Jodeci.

Q: Who are your biggest inspirations/your favorite writers?

A: I'm inspired by anyone who can construct art in such a way that I get lost in their madness and say, *Damn! I felt like I was right there inside that story/poem.* I have always been intrigued by Morrison, and I found Bukowski during a bad marriage I was going through when I was younger. Buk had guts and grit; he took me away quite often. I read the Beat poets a lot too during that time.

Right now, Catfish McDaris is on the nightstand. I'm also enjoying several of the poets from Crisis Chronicles Press like Dianne Borsenik, Kevin Ridgeway, D.R. Wagner, and Lana Bella; John Burroughs is an amazing poet himself and puts out top-notch products. I love the great John Dorsey's work. I love the work and words coming from Indigent Press, Damian Rucci, Charles Joseph, and B. Diehl. There are so many more great writers that I follow and enjoy that we would be here for a while if I tried to name them all, so I will end with Natasha Head and my lovely friend Bree. If you do not know Bree, read her!

Q: What time of day do you do most of your writing?

A: Usually it is limited to the evening time, except for Sundays and Mondays when I am not working at the Madhouse.

Q: Why do you write?

A: Because I have not found the ability to just say, *goddamn I'm done*, and stick to it. There are days when I think to myself that I am not going to write anymore, because it takes up so much of my time and begins to feel like a curse, but then it is that same day when I have a thought that lights me up inside, and I write the best piece that I have written in weeks. It's fuckin' twisted like that, brother.

Q: Do you have any favorite quotes from writers?

A: I have a lot of quotes that I enjoy, sure, but I am going to give you one that I ran across the other day. It is from, Little Rascals, by Charles Joseph:

"Because most dogs can smell a mean pile of shit from a mile away"

Q: What is one piece of advice you would give new/aspiring writers?

A: You are going to read writings from people, and think that those writings are pure shit, but understand there are people who will think that your writing is pure shit too. It's the beast, so just be yourself, write to write, kick ass, and don't give up.

Q: Do you have any published books/chapbooks you'd like to talk about?

A: My latest book of poetry is titled, In All These Naked Pictures Of Us. I enjoy it, brother. It is a glimpse; it is multiple mental snapshots developed in the corner of a darkroom from old and new pieces of my mind. The bad love, good love, ex-wives, ex-lovers, mistresses, failed suicide attempts, the madhouse, alcohol, and many more moments which fueled the belief that, this life is going to kill me, and I'll be dead before I am thirty-five, but the truth is that I am now thirty-six, and this life hasn't killed me yet. I look over my shoulder frequently though.

A Different Kind of Bad Taste

My being on a silver platter is a feast—carelessly
scratch and pick me apart.

Start at the bottom above my knees, but
leave my heart and hands to feel you chewing
on the pieces that even if you were starving,
near death, you could never fully swallow.

You never could—she never could—he never
could, so I just walk the streets of this life with
teeth marks and bruises, chewed and tattooed,
all over my skin. They don't go away.

They just spook the next person who may be
tempted to try; it's thwarting, because I have
become addicted to the thought of soft lips and
sharp teeth ripping at me and my mind.

I have the solution. I am going to become a writer.
I am going to hide inside and fantasize. Are your
lips wet? Mmmm, do you feel good too? Chew
harder, can you taste the flavor of my confliction?
Is it disgusting? Are you shouting to everyone
around you to never make the mistake you just
made?

If so, it is ok, remember that I am used to not fully

satisfying. You can spit me out into the piles of dirt that decorate the floorboards,

and we can consider all of this just good information.

Hybrid

because it
rains in Hell too;

we can grow
and sell
roses to all

the lovers like
us, on these
hot tar streets

for eternity.

Interview with Gary Glauber

Q: When did you start writing?

A: I started writing in grade school, with existential stories that often worried my teachers. As a voracious reader, writing was the natural and inevitable complement.

Q: Who are your biggest inspirations/your favorite writers?

A: I have had so many inspirations; it would be foolish to name only a few. This could easily be ten times as long, but off the top of my head: Shakespeare, James Joyce, William Faulkner, Raymond Carver, George Saunders, Don Delillo, Phillip K. Dick, Thomas Hardy, Marcel Proust, Haruki Murakami, Alice Munro, Hemingway, Fitzgerald, Salinger, James Tate, Jack Gilbert, Wallace Stevens, T.S. Eliot, David Foster Wallace, Picasso, Turner, Beethoven, Lennon, McCartney, Elvis Costello, Joni Mitchell, Andy Partridge -- and this barely touches upon the depth and breadth of it. Read, watch, listen, experience – inspiration is everywhere!

Q: What time of day do you do most of your writing?

A: I used to be a late night writer, but my teaching career has changed me into more of an anytime opportunist. It could happen at any moment, should the muse be visiting.

Q: Why do you write?

A: I am a storyteller at heart, and I choose to believe there is merit in sharing that activity with others.

Q: Do you have any favorite quotes from writers?

A: About a gazillion, actually, but here's one from Oscar Wilde (Lady Windermere's Fan): "We are all in the gutter, but some of us are looking at the stars."

Q: What is one piece of advice you would give new/aspiring writers?

A: Read and experience as much as you can. Be inspired by others. Imitate styles en route to finding what works best for you. Submit, and revise often. Keep your sense of humor and try not to let rejection discourage you. Keep writing. It's often a hard, lonely task. But real writers know it is what they have to do, regardless: change the world one word at a time.

Q: Do you have any published books/chapbooks you'd like to talk about?

A: Two, currently. My first full length poetry collection, *Small Consolations,* was published in 2015 by Aldrich Press. More recently, a poetry chapbook, *Memory Marries Desire*, was published by Finishing Line Press. Both of these are available at Amazon.com, and I do hope more will eventually follow.

Plan, Plane, Planet

That musical phrase began
the careful dialectic
between him and his subdued creator,
examining trivial mysteries
of supreme intermittency,
the familiarity of discomfiture,
the quietude of naked grotesquery,
the chords of dissonance arranged
to evoke happiness and trigger
honeyed moments of grace.
This is the ongoing quest,
the aching yearning
to understand beauty's lure,
agony of hesitant survival,
pain of attempting to capture
word-defying wonders
in this daily magnificent grind.
The moon rises reluctantly
as the middle bridge resolves
back to usual verse and chorus,
a subtle nuance carefully mastered
within this sweet, crazy existential dance
that still entangles us all.

Workshopper

And he breathes the false assumption:
infinite time a place wherein
he crafts phrases, hones words, masters
meter in this occupation of hazard.
Modernists mumble dead rhymes,
then turn and run,rather than be
affected, extended, emended.
He sees, senses, and aspires.
Adieu, kissing an illusion of truth,
capturing nuanced imperative
in curious ways, eagerly imagining
success as puzzled illumination.
Prince of process, each ensuing draft
outstretches, pulling and polishing
'til technique negates meaning,
and he begins to believe
artifice as experience,
this stale sheen as natural.

(First published in *Yellow Chair Review)*

Interview with Josh Dale

Q: When did you start writing?

A: I began my writing ventures around 13, writing my first poem about midnight, that is, that singular moment when time shifts from P.M. to A.M. I felt like it was quite intuitive and philosophical for my age (laughs). I began prose writing in the ensuing years, writing short fiction scenes that resulted in an ending that never arrived. In high school, I tried drawing and writing comics but never made anything of that either. I rediscovered writing in my adult life in 2012 when a novel idea struck me (to this day about 80% finished). From thereon, I've been writing consistently as I gain more knowledge of writing theory and reading a broad range of texts.

Q: Who are your biggest inspirations/your favorite writers?

A: The classics. American classics. I say that with the utmost confidence. The plights of the American artist in a land with no history, revealed a sort of 'savagery' deep within the psyche, hence bringing forth masterful works. I enjoy the Transcendentalists (Emerson, Thoreau, M. Fuller) when looking into critical thinking and theory. For writing technique, I enjoy Gothic stories by Poe and Hawthorne, to Wharton and Chopin, to Crane and Lovecraft and beyond. My belief is to write like a master, one must learn from a master. Lately though, I've been delving into international authors such as Bolaño, Kafka, Tolstoy, Camus, Aíra, and Hemmingway (if you consider him international, I do). So I'm a bit of a hypocrite, but that's okay. Emerson said it's ok to be inconsistent.

Q: What time of day do you do most of your writing?

A: It depends. Typically, I like to write between 9 PM-Midnight with a few beers at hand, but there are times when I do from 8-11 AM or even after 1 AM. I've been working two jobs plus full-time college for the past 2 years now, so free time is scant. Luckily, I have an hour plus commute on the train so I have opportunities to write/memo poetry or short story excerpts. I also take the time to visit the library and pen an hour-one and a half hours work when I can. As Ruth Stone once said, poems arrive 'like a thunderous train of air', so I always carry a notebook whenever that poem arrives.

Q: Why do you write?

A: This is the most loaded question to ever be asked in the literary world, so I will respond with the simplest answer first: I just have a way with words. Here is the more analytical answer: My adopted writing method is this. I write, for inside my head, is a whirlpool of ideas, and every now and then, one gets pulled through the spout which is my hand (odd image huh?). Sometimes they can be abstract, sometimes they are highly detailed, some are simply too convoluted to even give a passing glance. It's about 60% imagination, 40% observation, but the ratio varies, especially when I am out in Philadelphia or in a park.

Q: Do you have any favorite quotes from writers?

A: "To be great is to be misunderstood."

—Emerson

"All you have to do is write one true sentence. Write the truest sentence you know."

—Hemmingway

"It does not matter how slowly you go as long as you do not stop."

—Confucius (Not a writer, per say, yet I've followed this quote for years now. It has become a part of my psyche.)

Q: What is one piece of advice you would give new/aspiring writers?

A: I feel that I am not qualified enough to answer this question, but I will do my best. My advice, as a writer, is to just read, then write, then read twice as much, then write twice as much. I have grown to admire the brevity of short stories and poems opposed to the grandiose novel, but to each their own. Find a 'model' and emulate he/she/it as much as possible (mine was described in the second question). Lastly, on writing, become as humble as you must. *The chase for fool's gold shall turn pockets inside-out.* Make solid friendships and networks, brainstorm, workshop, etc. You can't assume you are writing The Next Great American Novel if you are the sole reader.

My advice, as a publisher, is to never sell yourself short for the sake of expediency. The birth of E-books and inspirational quotes has completely seized the artwork by the throat. The term 'dime novels' has become a monster, and that's not good. The design process must be in phases, and each phase has its pro's and con's. You will know how difficult it is to edit a 40 page chap for weeks, missing the same grammatical/punctuation error over and over. You will know what it's like sacrificing sleep for the correct trim size or emailing your designer at 1AM with a critical adjustment to the cover art. Plan from the beginning and things will pan out easily, in both idea and publication. *Take your time* and reap what you sow.

Q: Do you have any published books/chapbooks you'd like to talk about?

A: I have self-published two chapbooks under my imprint *Thirty West*. One is *The Being That Ensues From What Cannot Be Explained*, which is a short story with a non-standard trim size and format. The second, *Duality Lies Beneath,* is a perfect-bound chapbook which delves into my imagination as well as critiques of modern society and internal psychology. They are both available on Amazon Kindle format and print, however *The Being* can only be purchased through me via Paypal or Etsy, for it is a limited release. I see these two publications as the 'prodigal son' of my early writing career and hope that with these, my readership shall expand and possibly obtain a nod from the academia in which I thrive. To date, they have reached 4 continents and have almost ten reviews a piece. I try to keep track of all that purchase and thank them sincerely.

Grey

Space
Debris Hail-beaten façade
Run aground
Sever storm warning
Fulfills its name
In grey
Black hole
Serrated light
Columns topple
Power lines
Still
Retain
Charge

Interview with GothicGhetto

Q: When did you start writing?

A: I started writing sometime in middle school around the age of 11, but it wasn't until my freshman year of high school when I was told that I had a real talent for writing. In English class we had read Romeo and Juliet and for a class assignment we had to write a tragic love story. Mine was done so well my teacher wanted me to apply to the High School for the Performing and Visual Arts, unfortunately my father had me committed to a psych ward instead.

Q: Who are your biggest inspirations/your favorite writers?

A: I am generally inspired to write about life events, mostly my own and how I perceive the world. My all time favorite writer has always been Stephen King, I like how he can get inside your head and muck things up.

Q: What time of day do you do most of your writing?

A: I don't have a particular time of day to write, nowadays I am really busy with school but I keep a notebook handy to jot words down when they hit me then when I have a little free time I construct them into something more coherent.

Q: Why do you write?

A: Catharsis. There are a lot of messed up things in my head I am working to get rid of …

Q: Do you have any favorite quotes from writers?

A: The first line from Emily Dickinson's "Nobody knows this little Rose" which happens to be "Nobody knows this little Rose"

Q: What is one piece of advice you would give new/aspiring writers?

A: Write, write, write eventually it will turn into something worthwhile and besides it's good practice.

Q: Do you have any published books/chapbooks you'd like to talk about?

A: I have pondered the idea of writing a book/chapbook, but so far I have only had some poems published in Section 8 Magazine.

Programming

I live in a world
not of my choosing
constant battle
always losing ...

these be the thoughts
occupying my mind
wasting my time

waiting for the bus
to arrive ...

it's as if I'm conceived
without heaven's consent
that has me living hell bent

trapped within
this environment
that chooses for me
regardless of what works

diseased seeds that deceive
made to believe

I am thinking ...

things that make me
accept ways I am

resolving mental's pressure
through cognitive's dissonance
ego's bloated arrogance

memes clog my mind
infecting but can't see
because we're both blind

I become chaos
thrust amongst chaos
center's peace
become found
never lost

I practice compassion
for my fellow man
not because I have to
but because I can

learning from experience
taking long enough to get
what I put out in the universe

comes back as blessings
or severe curse ...

this is what I find
in what I do
returned in kind ...

The Way of Me

Tired of damn people always tryin' test me
Want me to be what they can't conceive
My head already wicked fucked up
Mind's binds got me blind
To the demon's infesting lies

Crawlin' blind I'm here
Always black
Light it lacks
Still just me
In this fucked up scene

Imprisoned in this
Tortured Mind State
Demons already been ate
What's left of my soul
In this fucked up
Dead ass Prison
Revolving Darkness
In a Never Ending System

Always been this way
What you don't believe
Talkin' out my ass
All this shit I say

Just livin' life – not me you see
Fucked up hopes
And shattered dreams
Livin' in this torn reality

Destroyed now gone
Words still lost

Of Broken Make Believe
Never knowin' what it
Truly Cost

The question that be, what's wrong with Me
Live my life, you don't want to see
Get inside my head will leave you Dead
With all the Dark Thoughts that I've said

In the Darkness where demons lay
It's like that from day to day
Til the night I'm dead and gone
Search for that Release
Is what I long

Interview with Don Beukes

Q: When did you start writing?

A: If I remember correctly, I actually used prose questions in a languages creative writing section from exams in high school during the latter part of the 1980's to have an excuse to let my imagination run wild. What was interesting is the fact that I was able to express myself creatively both in my first language, Afrikaans as well as my second language, English. I think that gave me the edge to go beyond my limitations. If it was not for my family who encouraged me to read more widely and visit the local library religiously, I would not have had the confidence to ooze out words on paper.

Regarding poetry, I am actually a late bloomer. I remember scribbling very short poems on pieces of paper in my early twenties and handed it out to close friends of mine. One title springs to mind, 'The Eagle' and for the life of me I don't know what happened to that piece of paper! It could be worth gold one day you never know hey? On a more serious note, I found myself grabbing a pen immediately after a break-in during a visit to my brother in South Africa in 2009 when I lived in the

UK. I was so livid and upset that I wrote a poem about it to also address rising crime at the time and it was subsequently published in 'Dissident Voice' last year.

Q: Who are your biggest inspirations/your favorite writers?

A: It goes without saying that I was quite affected by the writing of Nelson Mandela in his autobiography *Long Walk to Freedom*, which gave a raw, honest account of his journey to freedom and his determination to succeed against all odds. His integrity, fairness and intuition is very inspirational and his legacy will live on though his moral compass. I also like to read the works of Wilbur Smith, who captures the heart of South Africa over three centuries of international involvement in his sweeping sagas either on safari or on some voyage somewhere.

Also Tolstoy, Paul Glynn (*Song for Nagasaki*), Harper Lee, Shakespeare, Ingrid Jonker, André P.

Brink, Dave Pelzer, Stephen King, Roberto Bolano (*The Romantic Dogs*, 2000) and many others.

I would love to name current Indie poets out there who is a great inspiration to me but I might leave out a name by mistake and they know who they are.

Q: What time of day do you do most of your writing?

A: I tend to spill out words on paper late at night into the early morning, as I work part-time, especially when selecting which journals or magazines or anthologies to submit to.

Generally, I write down a word or phrase or name whilst watching a film or documentary or anytime a title forms in my mind.

Q: Why do you write?

A: When an emotion stirs in me or I get affected by the current state of humanity I feel moved to grab my notebook and capture a thought, a title, a feeling. Maybe I have never been given the opportunity to raise my voice for others to actually listen to what I have to say. For some reason my writing has become a spiritual journey, as I am starting to realize the power of words, images and themes which others can relate to and be uplifted, inspired, angered, liberated. I am not the master of my word weaving. I myself do not know what will flow out of me onto paper until the moment I write down the first word. It excites me, drives me, saturates me. That's why I write.

Q: Do you have any favorite quotes from writers?

A: Too many to mention but here are a few:

'As long as poverty, injustice and gross inequality persist in our world, none of us can truly rest' – Nelson Mandela

' No one is useless in this world who lightens the burdens of another' _ Charles Dickens

' Man is the cruelest animal' – Friedrich Nietzsche

'Anything too stupid to be said is sung' – Voltaire

'Hate the sin, love the sinner' – Mahatma Ghandi

Q: What is one piece of advice you would give new/aspiring writers?

A: When something from deep within you stirs you to write down a thought, an emotion, a warning or even a note to yourself, don't let go of that which comes from within at the right time or the right place in order for you to share your moral compass with humanity.

Q: Do you have any published books/chapbooks you'd like to talk about?

A: This will probably disqualify me but I have as yet not published a book or chapbook. I am waiting to hear from Erbacce prize 2016. I have however been successful in being included in my first Anthology publication, 'Shades of the Same Skin' published by Creative Talents Unleashed.

African Diva

I am the legend
of millennia my story

still epically
riddled with fear
at the dawn of time
my worth rather sublime
my gift to man painfully
a divine crime
instinct and intuition
my lifetime ambition
abused and violently
misused glorified in fiction
laws of man and land could
not break me even through
their scarlet imprints
they did not see
my earthly connection
created by atomic friction
my universal appeal
causing global
contradiction
I am still a pulsating
life-giving force
witness to senseless
and devouring
devastating wars.

My legacy
will be
historically
murmured
forever
I am and always
will be
African Diva.

(First published at The Poet Community)

Interview with Marianne Szlyk

Q: When did you start writing?

A: I've been writing off and on throughout my whole life. I remember dictating stories to my grandmother before I could write. She would write the stories in her perfect penmanship on the blank pages of *My Book House*, a twelve volume series of children's literature that had belonged to my father when he was a little boy. Since then I've written poetry, short stories, a novel or two, book reviews, letters, and many, many term papers. Actually, these days I mainly write poetry—and comments on students' papers.

After publishing a few poems in my twenties, I stopped writing for over twenty years. It's been five years since I've resumed writing poetry, by the way, and I hope that I can continue for many more because there is always something (some topic, some style) to explore.

Q: Who are your biggest inspirations/your favorite writers?

A: My inspirations change from summer to summer or winter to winter. (I mostly write during the summer and winter breaks as I prefer to concentrate on teaching during the school year.) Walking in my neighborhood and the nearby city of Washington DC inspires me. Music on YouTube and CDs, especially jazz but also rock music and oldies, inspires me as well. My husband and I attend concerts frequently, so I should add live music to the mix. I love to read biographies and memoirs and watch documentaries, so reading or hearing about other people's lives is another big inspiration. For a while, I would write poems about not-quite celebrities like Julie London or Dorothy Ashby, the Jazz Harpist. My cats also appear in my poetry. In fact, "Crepuscle with Callie" imagines that cat's nightmare: to live in a house with the Jazz Baroness' mob of cats. I tend to write more seasonal poetry although right now I am revising a poem set during this past winter's Snowzilla. I may also return to my Celtic astrology poems, too; these have been inspired by Martin Willits, Jr.'s poems on this theme. I am not a fan of astrology, but I love the idea of tree signs. Imagine being born under the sign of the hawthorn or the oak!

I also enjoy experimenting with form, although I began as a free-verse poet, inspired by Robert Lowell's Life Studies, Anne Sexton, Elizabeth Bishop (Jane Shore, one of my professors at Tufts, was a huge fan of Bishop's work), and the free-verse translations of Chinese poetry. Ever since I read Richard Wilbur's haiku sequence in Annie Finch's *An Exaltation of Forms*, I've been incredibly intrigued by that format. (My "We Disaster Tourists Travel to the Salton Sea" is in that format.) I don't think I will ever become a haiku poet as they are too short for me, but I really like using haiku as stanzas in my poem. Perhaps with time they will absorb some of the haiku spirit.

I am looking forward to exploring some new poets and spending time with old friends this summer. This past spring I attended the Split This Rock conference (which concentrates on poetry of social protest) in DC and came home with half a dozen books! Some are from a panel on eco-feminism that I attended. I am also reading Felino A. Soriano's new collected poems and learning from his approach to poetry, so different from my own. And I am looking forward to reading Catfish McDaris' collected poems and flash fiction. Perhaps they will inspire me to revive my sense of humor.

Q: What time of day do you do most of your writing?

A: I wish I could say that it doesn't matter, but I write new material in the morning and revise at night. I am trying to be more flexible. Overall, I am more of a night owl although my husband and our cat Thelma are working on trying to make me more of an early bird. In fact, right now, she is patiently waiting for me to shut down the computer and give her a midnight snack, which I do just before bed.

Q: Why do you write?

A: I write to be creative, to remember persons and places in my life, and to observe. I think of many of my poems as sketches. I have striven to write fiction, but I have a hard time with plot, specifically letting terrible things happen to my characters. So, instead, I write persona poems from a variety of viewpoints. Again these are sketches that allow me to write about places and persons I'll never be. Writing about oneself can be limiting and even frustrating since the literal truth and the figurative truth often clash or at least dispute with each other. I am fortunate that one of my most recent poetry teachers, Reuben Jackson, encouraged us to emphasize the truth of the poem, rather than the actual people and events.

Q: Do you have any favorite quotes from writers?

A: I'm afraid I don't really have a head for quotes, but out of the blue this afternoon as I was riding the bus home, Henry James' "try to be one of those on whom nothing is lost" popped into my head. I didn't even know that it was his quote till I googled it, but it epitomizes my ideal approach. Unfortunately, I can't google what Reuben Jackson used to say about poems having their own truth, but his words are still very influential to me.

Q: What is one piece of advice you would give new/aspiring writers?

A: Keep writing—and revising. I find that my poems constantly evolve and that they improve greatly from revision. Some poets may not revise much, but I rely on being able to remove what doesn't work and to add new material that may just take the poem in a new direction. Often I may even split poems when I am covering too much for one poem. Interestingly, to pick two poems, "In the Third Year of the Drought" (a short poem) and "Imagining Empathy" were once part of the same poem. However, I realized that I was trying to encompass too much, so I split the poem into two pieces.

Q: Do you have any published books/chapbooks you'd like to talk about?

A: Last fall Flutter Press published my chapbook *I Dream of Empathy*. I had been interested in the theme of empathy for a while, and I like writing poems from different people's perspectives. Around the time of Martin Luther King Day, the leader at a poetry group gave us the prompt to write about what it means to dream of empathy, a theme that I have always been very much interested in. Imagining the world from different perspectives was also relevant to my membership in that poetry group, given that the membership was predominately African-American. The poem that I wrote was "I Dream of Empathy," the first poem in the collection. I chose the other poems in the collection for the light that they shed on this quality. Another poem "Imagining Empathy" was inspired by my friend Bea Garth's painting *Empathy*. By the way, that painting is on the cover. A set of poems in the book juxtaposes the perspectives of three women in the same family: the dying grandmother, her pregnant granddaughter, and the bustling daughter-in-law/mother. I also included some personal poems as well, which helped me find more empathy for my mother and my first husband—although I must say that the trip he and I took in "Travels with the White Ghost" was incredibly stupid, perhaps the most stupid thing I have ever done in my life.

I Dream of Empathy is available on Amazon at http://www.amazon.com/I-Dream-Empathy-Marianne-Szlyk/dp/1517160677

I have another, earlier chapbook, *Listening to Electric Cambodia, Looking Up at Trees of Heaven.* It is an e-chapbook available through Kind of a Hurricane Press: http://barometricpressures.blogspot.com/2014/10/listening-to-electric-cambodia-looking.html. This collection has less of a theme although, I suppose, that music is one theme and multiculturalism may be another. The poems are a bit more quirky, too. One of them takes place at the Miracle of Science, a bar near MIT in Cambridge. Another is set at Ashley Stewart, a plus-size clothing store that I used to frequent. However, some are quite serious and beautiful, too.

I am strongly considering putting together another chapbook, this one emphasizing my experiments with counted verse and other forms. However, it will still include some free verse, as I continue to write in this vein.

We Disaster Tourists Travel to the Salton Sea

Last year's flowers stand,
sun-bleached kindling for the fire
about to happen here.

Blue sky flames, a torch
in the earth's hands. The sun is
the white-hot center.

No one smokes. Engines
do not idle. Air effaces
smells of death and life.

All that remains in
the sea's heart will never quench
the flames we wait for.

We wait, take small sips
of bottled water, then wait
some more. We tourists

Fly from disaster
to disaster, our quick flights
adding fuel to the flames.

Let's Go Away for Awhile

Thelma and her husband sing along to *Pet Sounds*
when driving to the Cape. Jerry Cole's guitar
begins "Wouldn't It Be Nice," and they launch

into song, his voice too wild, hers with
the Texas accent she never can lose. They
plunge in, splashing past strip malls and swamp.

But this instrumental is the song she loves best,
a vibraphone like sunshine against drums like surf,
a horn like the wave that crashes furthest

onto the rocks, not quite the highway.
The strings are clouds, meringue she has whipped
up in a stainless steel bowl at home.

She almost forgets that the east coast
has weak surf, and slimy seaweed clings to
 waders' calves in warm, knee-high water

as she and her husband waddle in among
the thin girls from Boston. She then remembers
cold, cloudy Mondays when the two of them

drive back home, listening to their inland music:
Chicago blues, Texas swing, "Honky Tonkin'"--
old songs that better suit their voices.

Maybe she likes that this instrumental comes before anyone can see the bridge or the traffic.
Or she likes to catch her breath.

Interview with Shelly Miller

Q: When did you start writing?

A: I found a short poem I had written about my grandma while in the 6th grade. Really though I didn't start until I was about 42. I was in the hospital for a mental illness. One of the groups was writing and I was encouraged by the facilitator to keep writing. It eventually evolved into writing poetry.

Q: Who are your biggest inspirations/your favorite writers?

A: People just starting out. People I've been reading on the poetry sites.

Q: What time of day do you do most of your writing?

A: I'd have to say often I end up writing when I can't go to sleep and then something takes hold and

I start to get phrases and snippets of ideas in my head. I then know I need to get up and write them down or I'll forget them. Many times it goes right into a poem then. Sometimes I'll wake in the middle of the night and do a little writing.

Q: Why do you write?

A: Writing helps me get things out of my head. Sometimes emotions, thoughts, ideas roll around and around in my head but once I put things on paper it can be a release and or help me put things in perspective. Seems these days writing poetry is constantly on my mind. I'm always looking for inspiration around me.

Q: Do you have any favorite quotes from writers?

A: "I'm taking up my cause again to be creative and free to be who I am." This is from Sharon Peters, a person I was in a group with.

Q: What is one piece of advice you would give new/aspiring writers?

A: Don't get discouraged. Not everyone is going to like your style just as you like some styles more than others. That's okay because what's coming from you is important to share. It's a gift to others. Keep writing and reading what others have written and you will only get better.

Grace

Leaves bend toward the light
Spreading open to the giving

Growing
I bend toward the hope
Opening my heart
That my life
May be worth living

Perhaps contentment was
Hidden behind the squall
That tormented my soul

Now with the sun shining
Maybe I can see the
Hope that was always there

My heart hidden in the
Grief of living
Grace can help me keep up
Hope
Contentment
Gratitude
Acceptance of who I am

Created in God's image

Interview with Wesley D. Gray

Q: When did you start writing?

A: One night when I was twelve as I was trying to sleep, there were just these words floating around in my head. I tried to ignore them, tried to find sleep. But sleep wouldn't come and the words wouldn't go away, so after what seemed like hours, I gave in. I got up, found a pencil and notebook paper, and scribbled them down. That night I wrote my first poem and I've been writing, more or less, ever since.

Q: Who are your biggest inspirations/your favorite writers?

A: Edgar Allan Poe, H. P. Lovecraft, Algernon Blackwood, Arthur Machen, Robert E. Howard, Joseph Payne Brennan. Those guys are all dead, of course. I would say my greatest *living* inspiration is currently Bruce Boston. If I could pattern myself after, and achieve even a fraction of the greatness of any one contemporary poet, it would be Bruce Boston.

Q: What time of day do you do most of your writing?

A: These days? Any time I can manage to scrape up. With work and family, it's the same old story, so I write in early mornings, when there's down time at work, or even while driving, dictating into my phone during my long commute.

Q: Why do you write?

A: Because I have to. Writing is my passion.

Q: Do you have any favorite quotes from writers?

A: "Art Harder Motherfucker." –Chuck Wendig. Sorry, you can edit that out if you want.

Q: What is one piece of advice you would give new/aspiring writers?

A: Just write.

Q: Do you have any published books/chapbooks you'd like to talk about?

A: I have this little chapbook, *Come Fly with Death: Poems Inspired by the Artwork of Zdzislaw Beksinski.* The title pretty much sums it up. It's a brief collection, but it's a work I'm really quite proud of. It's currently available on Amazon.com in print, and I sell signed copies through my website, www.wesdgray.com.

Bring the Light

What wretched creatures lie before me!
Squealing, squirming in the dark,
enthralled amidst their feasting orgy.

Gnashing teeth, spattering blood,
festering bone;
their tongues dance along the drips
of other men's pain.

A cryptic overseer
looms beyond the mist,
his crow shoulders
pecking upon the scars.

A thousand wicked grins
gleam from rubble and from rot,
a pile of waste—
dead men leering in the dark.

A door to freedom is at their backs,
but most will never see it,
long since trading eyes
for sharper teeth and larger maws.

But I bring the Light,
and I wear the shroud.
My candle burns;
my flame never falters.

The Bearer of the Cross walks beside me.
We pass among the throng

and it parts before our steps;
like the splitting seas—

I bring the Light

and the darkness scatters.

Interview with Bilkis Moola

Q: When did you start writing?

A: I began writing seriously in July 2011. While I might have dabbled in creative writing and poetry as a child /teenager, I did not commit to it as I regarded my efforts as mediocre and insufficient for development.

Q: Who are your biggest inspirations/your favorite writers?

A: Sylvia Plath remains my inspiration as her difficulty with relationships and her grievous crusade against depression embody the Achilles' heel within my poetry. Her suicide two weeks after the publication of her novel, *The Bell Jar* at the age of thirty-one has reached its 50th anniversary while *The Bell Jar* that was originally published under the pseudonym, Victoria Lewis has sold millions of copies globally. The woman who endured self-torment and would have been eighty-three years old today, tragically did not survive to realize her immense contribution to literature as well as her impact on the lives of millions of readers.

William Wordsworth's expression of "heightened perception" invigorates my creativity when scenically located while the poetry of Gerard Manley Hopkins galvanizes my use of alliteration. "Preludes" by T.S. Eliot in my now tattered copy of his *Collected Poems 1909-1935* is my most beloved possession.

I have an eclectic selection of favorite writers. Authors who inhabit my popular fiction shelf are Dan Brown and Gillian Flynn. I refer to Karen Armstrong for reference on world religion and Alain de Botton is my favorite contemporary philosopher. Malcolm Gladwell's "cultural commentaries and intellectual adventures" as depicted in his introductory biographies, satiate my thirst for non-fiction while David Nicholls' "One Day" and "Us" appeal to my escapades for the throes of love and the pitfalls of romance.

Q: What time of day do you do most of your writing?

A: My responsibilities as a Departmental Head at a senior-primary school severely encroach on my time to write therefore, I reserve Monday afternoons and evenings for the structured composition of my poetry. Nevertheless, I scribble images or lines rather spontaneously when inspiration beckons. This occurs most often before falling asleep when I will rise from my bed to note the thoughts floating in my mind.

Q: Why do you write?

A: I separated from my now ex-husband at the end of October 2010 after four years of an emotionally, verbally, psychologically and physically abusive marriage. The divorce was finalized in February 2011. The effects of divorce are traumatic and results in the processing of deep pain, the recovery of self-esteem/self-worth and the struggle to acquire a fresh, empowered identity with the need to face the future without bitterness and with positivity and hope. Writing poetry served as a refuge. The expression of emotion transferred through images upon paper allowed a catharsis to occur as healing materialized from the processing of my experiences and feelings.

The attempt for personal affirmation launched my identity as a poet. The writing of poetry is an active pursuit to document the observations of my interior and external landscapes. The appreciation of a breathtaking dawn or the glimpse of a magical sunset finds expression as the sensory and emotional arrest of images transferred onto paper. Perception weaved through language creates a structure for the flow of the thoughts and ideas that shape my psyche. The writing of poetry renders an envelope for my experiences and creates a shift in awareness through imaginative exploration.

Q: Do you have any favorite quotes from writers?

A: Maya Angelou's, "Still I Rise."

Q: What is one piece of advice you would give new/aspiring writers?

A: Heed the words by Alfred Tennyson, "To strive, to seek, to find and not to yield".

Q: Do you have any published books/chapbooks you'd like to talk about?

A: Yes. I have a published anthology of poetry that was launched and distributed throughout South

Africa in November – December 2013. This anthology remains available for sale as I host "Poetry As Therapy" workshops with various organizations that address the subject of abuse.

Wounds and Wings: A Lyrical Salve Through Metaphor is an anthology of poetry that is structured in three parts. The analogy of a caterpillar's transformation to a butterfly reflects the parallel process of personal transformation. Each stage of transition reveals the series of changes and events that emerge from introspection and unfold as a sequence of discovery and growth. This anthology is an exploration of the emotional pastures and wastelands that encompass the intimacy of celebratory and tragic human experiences as articulated in the figurative expression of poetry.

The Sensory Fairground

Love suffices in amiable magnanimity
for eyes entranced to reveal the story
of a soul arrested, feeble in gaze
captivated in heart by the beloved's visage.

Sinuous fingers tingle an impulse to touch
the graze of stubble and lips that brush
a candyfloss cloud of sweet submission
bathed in honey and serene contemplation.

When the wayfarer's path as a serenade is played
whistling tunes of romance through melodious days
-
Love's odyssey as an opera evolves
the pitch of passion in exquisite song!

Scented as perfume from the petal of a rose
is love's fragrance ferried to the seat of a soul -
Wrapped in a bouquet of amorous hues

love's presence in a balmy festoon.

Love requires not language to declare
the treasures and pleasures of sentimental flair.
Hush says love still in sound
relish the sensation of the sensory fairground.

Interview with Alyssa Trivett

Q: When did you start writing?

A: I started writing while I was finishing high school/the early years of college. I've always been into independent music and my love for writing stemmed from my love of lyrics. It also comes from my love of reading poetry.

Q: Who are your biggest inspirations/your favorite writers?

A: Recently, my favorite writers are Delmore Schwartz and Maya Angelou. Some of my all-time favorite writers are poet Carrie Fountain, Bono of U2, songwriter Dan Andriano (of Alkaline Trio), Charles Bukowski, Sylvia Plath, Donna Vorreyer, songwriter John K. Samson, songwriter Jesse Lacey, and the list continues on.

Q: What time of day do you do most of your writing?

A: I'm most awake at night, so naturally, that's when I tend to work on writing. I usually scrawl a few lines if I'm in a waiting room for some sort of appointment also.

Q: Why do you write?

A: I write because I love the challenge of piecing lines together. I'm very observant. Writing also helps declutter my head.

Q: Do you have any favorite quotes from writers?

A: "When I'm writing I feel like I've suddenly made myself company. You become your own guest" -Unknown

""Not writing is not good but trying to write when you can't is worse." -Charles Bukowski

"I think the tendency to assume an autobiography while reading a poem has to do with the intimate nature of poetry, especially narrative poetry. The yielding voice. But it bothers me sometimes because assumptions like these can cheapen the craft. On the other hand, many of my poems are about my experience of the world. In this sense they are autobiographical. Still, material alone doesn't make a poem." -Carrie Fountain

"Time is the school in which we learn, time is the fire in which we burn." -Delmore Schwartz

Q: What is one piece of advice you would give new/aspiring writers?

A: This may sound generic, but let the material come naturally. It can't be force-fed, or else you'll sit there staring at a blank cursor [or page, etc.] for longer, versus letting the lines spill out themselves.

Q: Do you have any published books/chapbooks you'd like to talk about?

A: Currently, no, but you never know what the future holds!

For a Cup of Coffee

I'm adjacent to large signs,
cream colored paint, public restroom odor
trying to knock me out. Smelling salts.

A terrified reflection of my face
on metal panels of vending machines;
faint lettering appears from a former pay phone's
home.

I dodge, duck, dip, dive and dodge through—
a former voice I knew, but can't place.
Perhaps, the tenth grade gym teacher—
barking off orders, calling us
by our last names.

I'm seasick, a bike messenger weaving through
patterns of traffic. My sleeve is a basketball,
tipped from a hipster's messenger bag.

Everything is light and sound.
Blaring music of nineties one-hit wonders
Dirty snow hangs around,
forty degrees and faded lines on sidewalks.

Latitude and longitude
stairs stacked, elevators,
strollers and children. All I see
are structures.

I'm a traveler with a destination,
the ticks of tocks of a watch
begging to be raced against—

with no rush intact.

A stranded form of sunlight
dances off parked cars,
elevated doors open without
the public transportation voiceover.
And I'm off.

Interview with Rebecca Cherrington

Q: When did you start writing?

A: About 4 years ago but only just started properly sharing them!

Q: Who are your biggest inspirations/your favorite writers?

A: I love Rudyard Kipling and I'm also a fan of Mr Allan Poe! I am also a fan of Blaq Ice.

But I like new poets that are just getting known like yourself and A lady called Nadine Jessel.

Q: What time of day do you do most of your writing?

A: Normally at night when my two boys are asleep! Or at random times during the night when an idea wakes me up!

Q: Why do you write?

A: Writing is my therapy it helps with my depression and dealing with everyday issues.

Q: Do you have any favorite quotes from writers?

A: "we loved with a love that was more than love" Edgar Allan Poe

"All that we see or have seen is but a dream within a dream" Edgar Allan Poe

"if you can dream but not let the dream be your master" Rudyard Kipling

Q: What is one piece of advice you would give new/aspiring writers?

A: Write with your heart not your mind. If you're not passionate about it don't do it as it will be your mistress!

Q: Do you have any published books/chapbooks you'd like to talk about?

A: Yes I self published a book of poetry called Rainbows Appear of which all 25 copies were sold! I am currently saving up to do another. I also have a blog on which I write all my poetry.

www.sh1thappensandrainbowsappear.wordpress.com

I also have an online radio show on which I promote other poets it's on RedShift Radio on mix cloud and is called The Write Composition.

Writer's Tears

If I could sell writer's tears
Amassed over a couple of years
I would be rich beyond compare!
The frustration, tears the vacant stare
The emotional journey writers share
Whether it's for a hobby or that illustrious deal
The huge roller coaster of feelings writers feel!
The ups and downs, the twists and turns
The recognition we all yearn
The total and utter shock
If we can't overcome writer's block!
But we carry on through thick and thin
No matter how often we begin
If the passions there the words will flow
Even if sometimes it's quite slow!
The amount of tears we writers amass
We are a league of our own in our class!
It's worth the stress and pain believe me
Seeing your book in front of thee!

Interview with Layanne Aman

Q: When did you start writing?

A: At the age of 6, although back then, it was just random words strung together. I wrote my first poem at the age of 9 and had it published in a school magazine at age 10.

Q: Who are your biggest inspirations/your favorite writers?

A: I get inspired by nature, it is the go to standard inspiration of my life. People-wise, it started because of my sister reading Enid Blyton to me. At the age of 6, Enid Blyton's 13 year old self writing stories was nothing short of a miracle to me.

Q: What time of day do you do most of your writing?

A: Nights mostly. Or early mornings. Or sunsets. Basically any extreme emotion sets me off to pen them down.

Q: Why do you write?

A: Writing is a release for me, a release for the thousand words that keep going on in my head at all times. If I don't write, they jumble up in my head and block everything out. It's more like they (my thoughts) write by themselves, I'm just their means to an end.

Q: Do you have any favorite quotes from writers?

A: "Words are a lens to focus one's mind" - Ayn Rand

"Old age forgets what it feels like to be young" from Jk Rowling's character - Albus Dumbledore.

Q: What is one piece of advice you would give new/aspiring writers?

A: There is no advice needed for someone who wants to write. It's an art that begins to possess you, simply let go.

Q: Do you have any published books/chapbooks you'd like to talk about?

A: I've only published individual articles, and that was before I got into medicine. Being a doctor took away the time for me to pursue publishing, but the material I have saved up is surprisingly much.

If a Facebook page counts, then:

https://www.facebook.com/ThePoetSo/

Hopelessness

Dark heart, like the soot-gray of the sky,
Where all lost souls run wild,
Fretting, seeking what they could not find,
Upon the earth, among soulless mind.
To light a flame without love,
No fire, no fuel to burn it steady all night long,
Lost beyond the hope to salvage,
Frozen and empty, too forlorn.
Alas, the morning light shall soon
Burst through your deepening black within
And pierce through the midnight gloom
A ray of pure light, and warmth sink,
Yet so thoughtlessly you stay away,
And are gone before the sunshine bloom.
~So

Interview with Robert Wilson

Q: When did you start writing?

A: When I was around 15 or 16

Q: Who are your biggest inspirations/your favorite writers?

A: A video game called Max Payne is what got me into writing, actually. My main influences are Charles Bukowski, Henry Rollins, Ted Hughes, Robert Lowell, and Anne Sexton. Lyrics and music influence me greatly as well: Every Time I Die, Pig Destroyer, Bob Dylan, Tom Waits, Metallica, Sorority Noise, The Hotelier…

Q: What time of day do you do most of your writing?

A: Usually early evening or late at night.

Q: Why do you write?

A: Catharsis

Q: Do you have any favorite quotes from writers?

A: Lots

"Some people never go crazy. What truly horrible lives they must lead"
-Charles Bukowski

"Scar tissue is stronger than muscle tissue. You're turning me into scar tissue. I don't know if I should thank you or myself."
-Henry Rollins

"Once upon a time there was a boy who loved a girl, and her laughter was a question he wanted to spend his whole life answering"
-Nicole Krauss

"Love is unmistakable and nobody loves you like the one who waits."
-Keith Buckley

Q: What is one piece of advice you would give new/aspiring writers?

A: Don't. But if you must, have a mental meltdown or two. It helps.

Q: Do you have any published books/chapbooks you'd like to talk about?

A: My poetry collection, Houses I've Died In, is reaching its 1st birthday. It's autobiographical and confessional and I put a lot into it. You can check it out here:

https://www.amazon.com/Houses-Ive-Died-Robert-Wilson/dp/1515233731

I Can't Party With You Anymore

Lying in the gutter you pushed me in
whenever you were bored,
I can feel some kind of
inflamed rebirth
slowly breaking through my left wrist.
I welcome whatever happens
even if you never notice.
Perfection once coursed through your bones
where blemishes now stumble
like divorced drunkards.
You had love dripping from your lips
and then apathy bleeding
from your fingertips.
I tasted then both with a smile
as I admired your tiara of wasps
and the welts they left.
In and out,
admiration blossomed from every clock
when we were together
but time was not long for you.
I am now the speck of dust
you wipe from your glasses
as an afterthought
and I deserve so much more.
You can drink your narcissism
from a beer bottle.
I'll be stone sober,
weary of seeing your face
in every damned blurry object,
because it will kill me
and I deserve to live
a lot more than
I deserved any of this.

Scarlet Brilliance

If I knelt at your door
with seeds in my hair
would you pluck and plant them
in the Eden of your smile?
I've spent so much time running
from my own breathing patterns
that I couldn't hear you shouting at me to stop
so I wouldn't collapse.
I'll grow to believe I'm worth it
if you have the time,
I'll gladly soak up everything you teach me in
lonely mornings of static.
Watch me become invincible because of it.
We can sit on your living room floor
and fill in the colorless planets,
sign them as a gift to each other
to keep in our back pockets
in case of duress.
I remember when you held my pinky
on the day my neighbor killed himself
and lost yourself in my pulse.
You told me it was one of most beautiful things
you've witnessed
as your face flushed with a lunar eclipse
and pruned.
I wiped the rain away
and thanked you for everything,
watching how even this
couldn't dent your grace.
Do you know that if you tripped
over a stray, rabid thought
that I would hold you like a muse

and take every poisonous bite
until it died of exhaustion?
I hope so.
With all these days of crying and
laughing and
salvation they're bound to talk of us
in their sleep
as they dream of pure ice
and forests that stretch from here
to the edge of the world.
Walk there with me.

Interview with Ahmad Alkhatat

Q: When did you start writing?

A: When I was around 10 years old.

Q: Who are your biggest inspirations/your favorite writers?

A: My biggest inspirations are women's beauty and nature's beauty as well, and also the story of my first love, who made me a good lover and good writer. Honestly, I have no favorite writers or poets, since I believe they all write poetry in their own way, which make it hard for me to say to choose one or another.

Q: What time of day do you do most of your writing?

A: Usually late at night, when I see the moon and talk the unseen spirits, who I always feel I am talking to them in my poems.

Q: Why do you write?

A: Just to releases my stresses and depression inside of me.

Q: Do you have any favorite quotes from writers?

A: Not really…

Q: What is one piece of advice you would give new/aspiring writers?

A: Don't give up on writing, you may write nonsense proses at the beginning, but slowly, slowly creativity arises up in your mind, and above all keep reading short stories, poems, novels up.

Q: Do you have any published books/chapbooks you'd like to talk about?

A: Soon hopefully.

I Sat Next to My Life...

I sat next to my life, on the invisible chair of hopelessness.

As if one angel was sleeping sleeping on my shoulders.

I was staring at my life, recalling of the great memories,

They were so remarkable, that my life asked what happened?

What happened to the lover, who described love in depth?

What happened to the friend, who stood behind his fears?

What happened to the dreamer, who never gives up of dreaming?

I said, the lover died, after he refused to pay the homeless,

To buy a rose for his beloved, and said I'm saving my coins

To my death ceremony, I have a date in heaven with angels.

And about that friend, he disappeared behind the dark clouds.

Once he discovered of the sprites plan, to break his heart to fly off.

Once he cried, and flow his soul free, where flesh caught him.

The dreamer lost himself in between the dreams, and his nightmares

Of others lovers, by waking up with a flow of rhymes to write them as

If they were his own, he was lost when his life betrayed him, with death.

My life looked at me again, and cried hard of missing my long and weird

Answers, said why did you die way earlier, then your enemies should off.

I looked at her with laughter face, this life was created to the fools and

Not for poets, who writes with honest feelings but lonely with depressions.

My hair and, my face might look young, but my soul and heart were twice

Older then my actual age, which explains why no women wanted to date me.

Who can recover all the years, I was awake like the moon thinking of how

Tomorrow would be, if I am lonely with active hand writing, and dry kissing lips.

Even the pen gave up of writing, and stopped but I didn't give up on me

Last poem, and county to write it with my real blood by cutting my two arms and die.

I Have Created My Paradise

I have finally created my paradise,
With your loyal love, and my deep faith loving you.

No more miseries, or dark thoughts.
I reborn my heart thirsty to your God self beauty.

Hold my hands, until the sun sets down
where you and I get younger to cuddle like two
birds.

Let me make a gate that will open to the
messenger, who will write us joyous long lives.

This earth has made us atheists, sinners.
Where I stabbed myself to impress the heartbreaker.

Your black colour long curly hair will be
the tree of tears to hide all of my long untold stories.

They will not be four of confusing seasons,
Just by thinking of you, it gives a pleasure to the
day.

I will use your happy tears, to plant more of
jasmines.
I will use my emotional tears to make a sweet
winery.

I will use your grief's tears, to plant more flowers.
I will use my feelings tears, to make a taste to the lips.

Your two eyes will be of clearest blue heaven,
Where all of humanities are able to kiss you in the air.

In the day, you are going to raise up higher than
The sun shines, so I could kiss the lips of the morning.

In the night, I will be the sailor exploring your life.
Kissing and embracing your body, until you melt down.

Where your pink perfume will tag my hairy chest,
And slowly you will be the naughty and loving shining star.

Oh I know nothing is easy to stop us from our habits,
But the truth I cannot lie because I really love you from the soul.

The time will stop if you decide to walk away from me,
And my paradise will turn into the hell of all the sinners alone.

Nothing is more appreciate than you sitting next to

me,

Enjoying a dream of wishing to have created my paradise before.

About The Editors

Adam Levon Brown

Adam Levon Brown is a published author, poet, amateur photographer, and cat lover. He is an editor at Creative Talents Unleashed and a book reviewer for Five 2 One Magazine. He has been published in dozens of venues, including Burningword Literary Journal and Yellow Chair Review. Adam Levon Brown burst through the door of contemporary poetry in early 2015 after being diagnosed with Schizoaffective disorder. He used writing as a tool for catharsis and eventually started submitting his poems to journals and magazines. Now an established poet with dozens of publications, a fiction novella, and two full collections of poetry out, he plans to take the poetry world by storm. Adam is currently putting together several chapbooks and collections of poetry while aiming his sites at a poetry prize sometime in the future. He is also owner of Madness Muse Press, a super small independent press run out of Eugene, Oregon, which is working on publishing an anthology including interviews with poets from around the world. He attends Lane Community College and will soon attend the University of Oregon as an English Major/Creative Writing Minor.

Claudine Nash

If Claudine Nash were to answer some of the interview questions posed to the poets in *In So Many Words,* she would say that Paul Simon and e.e. cummings were her first poetic loves. She loves to wake up before the sun rises and walk the dog when the neighborhood is silent. It's during the early morning hours that most of her poems start to swirl and take shape. She writes because she feels incomplete when she doesn't.

Her formal bio would say that she lives and writes in New York where she is also a practicing Clinical Psychologist. Heavily influenced by her background in psychology, Claudine's poetry frequently delves into such topics as loss, healing and the liberation of releasing the past.

Her previous collections include her full-length poetry book *Parts per Trillion (*Aldrich Press, 2016) and her chapbook *The Problem with Loving Ghosts* (Finishing Line Press, 2014). Her poems have won prizes from *Avalon Literary Review, Eye on Life Magazine, Lady Chaos Press*, and *The Song Is...* and have appeared in numerous magazines and anthologies including *Asimov's Science Fiction, Cloudbank, Haight Ashbury Literary Journal* and *Yellow Chair Review* amongst others. You can read more about her poetry at her website www.claudinenashpoetry.com.

www.ingramcontent.com/pod-product-compliance
Lightning Source LLC
Chambersburg PA
CBHW060319050426
42449CB00011B/2556